THE MAD®
BOOK OF HORROR STORIES,
YECCHY CREATURES,
AND OTHER NEAT STUFF

WRITTEN BY **Lou Silverstone**
ILLUSTRATED BY **Harry North**

EDITED BY **Nick Meglin**

WARNER BOOKS

A Time Warner Company

WARNER BOOKS EDITION

Copyright © 1986 by Lou Silverstone, Harry North and
E.C. Publications, Inc.

All rights reserved.
No part of this book may be reproduced without permission.
For information address:
E.C. Publications, Inc.
485 Madison Avenue
New York, N.Y. 10022

**Title "MAD" used with permission of its owner,
E.C. Publications, Inc.**

This Warner Books Edition is published by
arrangement with E.C. Publications, Inc.

**Warner Books, Inc.
666 Fifth Avenue
New York, N.Y. 10103**

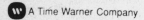 A Time Warner Company

Printed in the United States of America

First Printing: August, 1986

Reissued: September, 1991

10 9 8 7 6 5 4 3

CONTENTS

To MATT,

Who shares the blame for this book
for making me watch all those
horror movies!

LDS

FOREWARNED

Of all the horror tales told in recent years, perhaps the one that revolted MAD paperback readers most was the one that teamed the creature who writes (Lou Silverstone) and the beast who draws (Harry North) with the maniac who edits (Nick Meglin). Experts on the supernatural don't often agree on anything, but they are totally in agreement that these three are neither super nor natural in any way, shape or form!

Lou Silverstone was created one dark, stormy night in a drafty laboratory in Plainfield, New Jersey (a state noted for pollution, waste, and garbage). Following a 3-year stint in the US Army (Corpse Corps), Lou attempted to study at the University of Illinois—but they studied him instead! He later married the ghoul of his dreams and moved to Long Island where together they created Monster Matthew. Suburbia rotted what little was left of Lou's brain, which left him no choice but to write for MAD (a magazine noted for pollution, waste, and garbage).

Harry North, like Jack the Ripper, was the product of an English upbringing! Born with "ink in his veins," Harry worked on his first professional art assignment at age fifteen. Since he didn't get another assignment until he was eighteen, Harry abandoned his profession for several years, serving in the British Air Force where he rose to the rank of Full Moon each month. Returning to civilian life, Harry created specialized fast-food chains for fellow creatures— "Chicken-in-the-casket," "Vampire stake," "Mummy Mia Meat Balls," etc. Realizing that if "man can't live on bread alone," a wolfman can't live on the un-dead alone, either! So Harry returned to the commercial art world, designing running shoes for Big Foot and snow shoes for the Abominable Snowman. Noting that this area of design was also limited, Harry found work at Mad, feeling very much at home in the company of blood-sucking publisher Bill Gaines and sadistic tennis-playing editor Nick Meglin.

The retch is history...

GEFILTA-
THE KILLER CARP

SOMEWHERE OFF CONEY ISLAND...

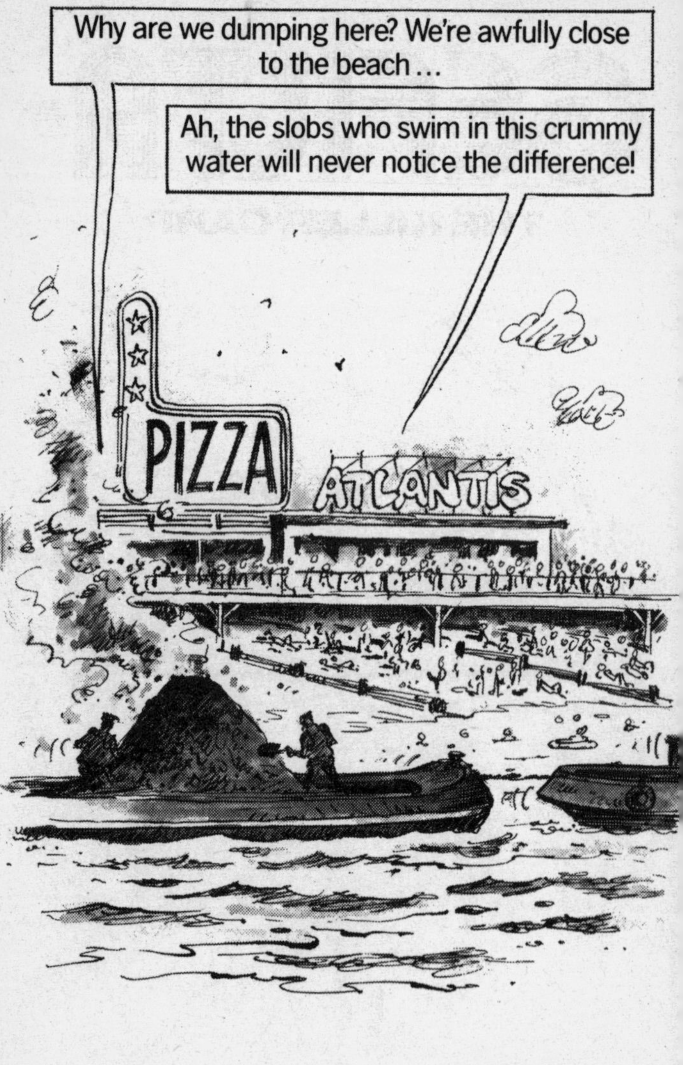

You'd think a mugger'd be satisfied taking the poor slob's wallet, his gold chain, his radio! Those he left! It's a **real** sickie who takes a guy's arms and legs!

What type of a **nut** are we dealing with, Doc?

Don't **flounder** about trying to catch this murderer, Lt.! This may seem **fishy,** but this man was killed by a **fish!**

Holy mackerel! Was it a **shark?**

14

15

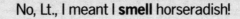

But the monster killed 4 people at last count!
Who cares! **People** aren't on the **endangered list!**
Watch out!

27

This is a mold of the creature's teeth made from the victim's wounds…
Amazing! It **does** resemble the teeth of the gefiltus!
This is probably unimportant, but there was an odor of **horseradish** on all the bodies!
Unimportant? Horseradish to a **gefilta** is like woods to a **bear!**

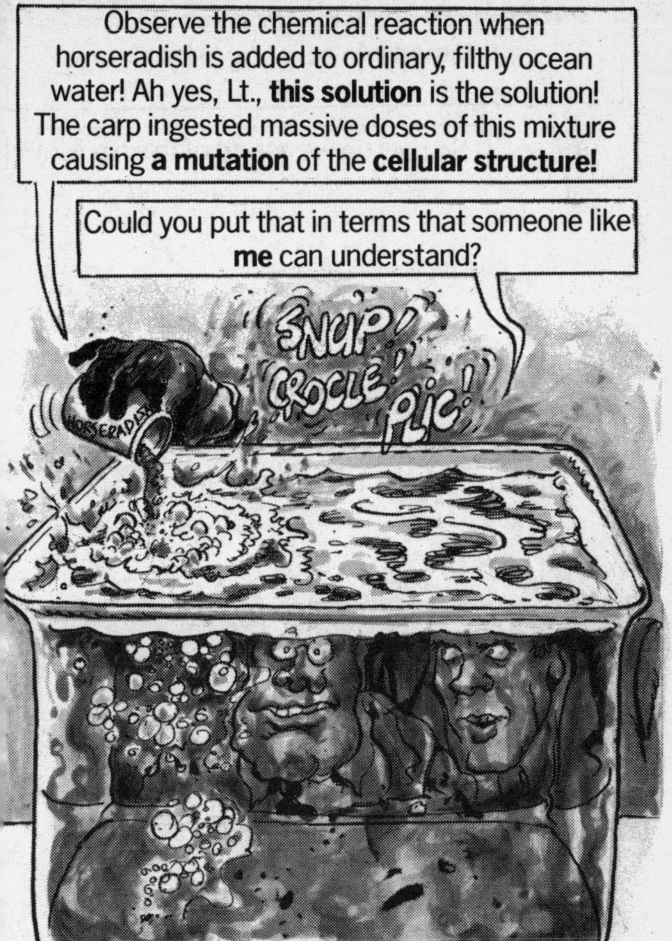
Observe the chemical reaction when horseradish is added to ordinary, filthy ocean water! Ah yes, Lt., **this solution** is the solution! The carp ingested massive doses of this mixture causing **a mutation** of the **cellular structure!**
Could you put that in terms that someone like **me** can understand?
SNUP!
CROCLE!
PLIC!
HORSERADISH

35

37

Don't you hate...

... when the nerds run to the **one** place where they're sure to be **trapped** ?!!

41

... when the **creature** starts getting sensitive and mushy instead of doing what he's **supposed** to be doing: killing, terrorizing, tearing people apart piece by piece?

... seeing a **dubbed** horror flick where the English they speak is more ridiculous than if they left it in the original Japanese?

... when some scientist tries to save the alien from outer space, even though he's already killed-off half the town and is about to start on the other half?

When that sucker steps on these **wires**, throw the switch! That'll barbeque him good!

What's to **learn**?..

49

... when the slop they're serving in the school cafeteria reminds you of the **blood** and <u>guts</u> you saw in the horror flick the night before...

...and the guy sitting next to you **agrees** with you, only he has less control of his barf impulses?

... when you succeed in not letting your girl see that you're scared for the whole film, and just when you think it's over, suddenly a hand comes out of the **grave** and you scream like an idiot?

... when the killer is stabbed, shot, burned and drowned and then reappears in the sequel?

That's the end of Druid! **Nothing** can survive in that **acid bath**!

WATCH FOR ARBOR DAY III
The Return of Druid

THE CURSE of the WEREWOLF

But—later in the night...

67

We see *all kinds* of horrible monsters on our movie and TV screens—creatures that come from outer space, from the swamp, spawned by nuclear explosions, mutations, man-made monsters, freaks of nature, even creatures grown in pods! But the *most terrifying* monsters of all are …

The CREATURES that come from the HEADLINES

MURDERS 11 O

SUB KILL

SOB ON NIRV! GRUESOME SHOW TONIGHT

Teenager's mutilated body found — key witness slain—

69

72

73

You sly devil, you! How **about** this guy, folks?
Yeah! Zap-a-rooty! Dig it!

Who do you want to play **you** in the film?

Burt Reynolds! At first I wanted **Redford,** but he's too blonde! We want the movie to be **realistic.**

Has being a **famous murderer** made much of a difference in your life?

You'd better believe it! Like, I could **never** get any chicks to go out with me, you know what I mean? Now I get **tons** of mail—all from broads—and lots of them want to **marry me!** Some of them send me letters with real off-the-wall proposals that I can't even talk about on TV! I tell you, Nirv, there's a lot of **sickies** in this world!

A MAD LOOK at DRACULA

THAT HOUSE IN VOMITY VILLE

97

the Fall of the House of Gusher

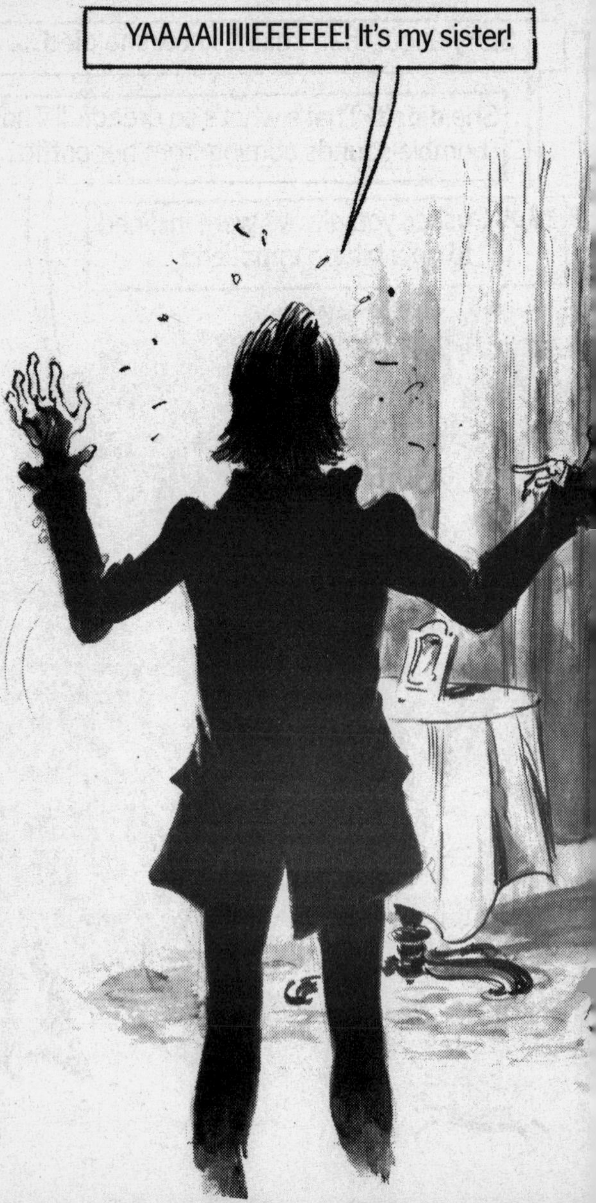
YAAAAIIIIIIIEEEEEE! It's my sister!

115

I'm afraid you're looking at the **last** of the Gushers, not to mention that the **house** is in worse shape than **we** are! Yes, my friend, the House of Gusher is doomed! Doomed! Doomed! How many "doomed" was that?

Three I believe!

Thank you! It takes at least **four** to make a dramatic point! May I?

117

The MAD Case of Dr. Jackyl and Mr. High

PROLOGUE:

This previously unpublished manuscript is the actual case history of Dr. Jackyl and Mr. High as recorded by his/their psychiatrist, Dr. Sigmoid Fraud, a member of the well-respected school of analysis, "Shrinks 'R' Us!"

Dr. Fraud left instructions that this paper was not to be published before the year 1885. However, no reputable publisher had the level of bad taste needed to publish the work until this edition.

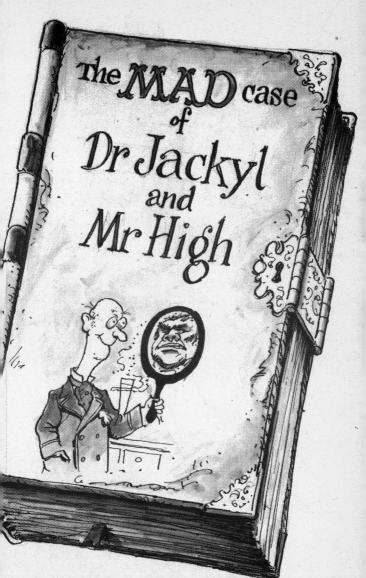

The MAD case of Dr Jackyl and Mr High

Chapter I

A NEW PATIENT

I will never forget the first time I had the misfortune to lay eyes on the evil personage known as Edward High! I was in my office with a patient, an accountant named Sydney Loophole. Mr. Loophole was suffering from the delusion that people found him boring. I was suddenly awakened by a terrifying scream that came from my waiting room. "I'm afraid our time is up, Mr. Loophole," I informed him.

"Am I making progress?" he inquired.

"Indeed you are, old chap," I replied, "why I didn't fall asleep for almost ten minutes today!"

I ushered him out a rear door and hurried back to my waiting room. There I witnessed a most disgusting sight. A short, repugnant man in ill-fitting clothes was chasing my receptionist, Miss Ample! It was obvious he was trying grab her ample bum!

"Sir," I snapped curtly, "this isn't a massage parlour, it's a doctor's office!"

He stopped his pursuit, gave me an evil glance and snarled, "Well, I'm playing doctor!"

I ordered him to leave my office immediately or I would call the police! "Yer a shrink, aintcha? I got a problem. I know it's hard to believe, but people don't like me."

Chapter II

MEET EDWARD HIGH

My new patient sat down on the couch and said his name was Edward High.

"What gives you the impression that you're not liked?" I inquired.

"Well," he replied, "when I go into a singles bar, it really becomes a singles bar! Everybody leaves and I'm left there alone. If they put my face on a stamp people would spit on the wrong side. What has that twit Dr. Jackyl got that I ain't?"

I was taken aback by this. What could my friend and colleague Dr. Jackyl have to do with this fiendish creature? I said, "Do you mean Dr. Henry Jackyl? Well, he's a lovable, generous, kind gentleman!"

"Besides that!"

" Jackyl is polite, well educated, charming, witty, and he's a swell dancer!"

High snapped, "Maybe I ought to spend my time at a dance studio insteada' some bloody shrink's!"

I showed High some ink blots and asked him to identify them. He became extremely excited. "Ah," he said, "that one's a bloke getting his ruddy throat slit! That one's a creep with his brains bashed in! That's a fat lady gettin' trampled on by a horse—or maybe it's a horse gettin' trampled on by a fat lady! Got any more? I like this game!"

127

Chapter III

THE ILL FITTING SUIT

"Mr. High, why did you hate your mother?" I asked.

"I didn't hate my mother," he replied.

"Mr. High, why did you hate your father?" I asked.

"I didn't hate my father," he replied.

"Sir," I said, trying to control my anger, *"I can't help you if you won't cooperate. It's a well known fact in the world of psychoanalysis, that everybody hated their mother or their father and in most cases both."*

"Schmuck," he hissed, *"I didn't have no bloody mother or father. But if it'll make your day, if I had I would have hated them. And I ain't too fond of you, neither!"*

"Do you hate Dr. Jackyl?"

His evil eyes lit up, *"Bingo!"* he cried, *I hate that wimp. I wish I could find a way to get rid of him permanently."*

"And why do you hate Dr. Jackyl?"

He smashed his heavy cane on my desk. *"I can give you a million reasons. For openers look how his damn suit fits me!"*

I gave him the name of my tailor and told him his time was up. He paid me by check and to my utter amazement, the signature on the check was that of Dr. Henry Jackyl!

Chapter IV

THE EVENING STROLL

That evening I decided to take a stroll to sort out the disturbing events of the day. Why did High wear Jackyl's clothes? And when he did, what clothes did Jackyl wear? As I walked and pondered, I chanced to meet F. Lee Bailiff, my solicitor. Maybe I could get some free advice on a pending malpractice suit.

"Bailiff, you old barrister," I greeted him. "I'm glad we met. I'm having a bit of a legal problem. One of my patients is suing me for malpractice. The chap is an alleged artist and it seems his lady friend asked him to cut off his ear to prove that he loved her."

"Good Lord," uttered Bailiff, "of course you told him it was out of the question."

"No," I replied, "I wanted him to make that decision for himself. I said, 'Vincent, do whatever you think is right.' Anyway, he cut off his ear and he maintains he can't paint anymore because his eyeglasses keep falling off."

"Look at the bright side, old chap," said Utterson. "You could have been in more serious trouble if, instead of an ear, she asked him to cut off..."

Suddenly a short figure appeared out of the swirling evening fog. It was Edward High!

Chapter V

A CHANCE ENCOUNTER WITH MR. HIGH

Utterson and I both doffed our hats in a gentlemanly greeting. High hit us both up along side our heads with his heavy cane and scampered away in the darkness.

I rubbed my aching head and mused, "I wonder what he meant by that?"

"That chap must have been an American. They're terribly rude, you know." said Utterson.

"No," I replied, "that was Edward High. He's a close acquaintance of our mutual friend, Dr. Jackyl.

"Of course, I thought that suit looked familiar," said Utterson. "Do you know Jackyl changed his will and is leaving his estate to High?"

"No," I chuckled, "could you hum a few bars?"

I felt a sudden, sharp pain in my head and I found myself on the ground. Standing above me was Mr. High brandishing his cane. His face was contorted with rage. "If there's one thing I can't bloody well stand, it's stupid old jokes!" he snarled and stormed off.

I watched as High disappeared into the fog and I sighed, "Everybody's a critic!"

Chapter VI

THE DISAPPEARANCE OF DR. JACKYL

I was worried about Jackyl. He had failed to show up for our weekly Trivial Pursuit game. I made inquiries and nobody had seen him for a fortnight. Jackyl had simply vanished.

When the obnoxious Mr. High arrived at my office for his session, I confronted him. "Where is Dr. Jackyl?" I asked.

"I'm looking for him too," he sneered. "See, we're playing hide and seek and he's hiding." High then leaned upon my couch and shouted, "Anybody around my base is it!"

"Mr. High, what have you done with my dear friend, Dr. Jackyl?"

He turned that dreadful smile on me and hissed, "Do you really want to know the truth about Dr. Jackyl and Mr. High?"

I nodded yes. High opened the small black bag he carried. From it he took some vials and envelopes of chemicals. He measured the chemicals and put them into a glass. The mixture gave off a bubbly vapor...pop ...pop...fizz...fizz...snap...crackle... POP!

High raised the glass to his lips. "Jackyl and I shared a drink," he said, "and then he split, hahaha." He drank the steaming concoction in one gulp!

Chapter VII

JACKYL'S DREADFUL SECRET

I will never forget the terror of the next few horrible minutes. High gasping for breath, clutching his throat as he staggered and reeled. His face darkened and his very features seemed to melt. He cried out, "My body's all aching and racked with pain!" Then he lurched against the table to steady himself. Finally the trembling stopped, he straightened up slowly, turned and standing before me was Dr. Henry Jackyl.

He smiled weakly and said, "You were expecting maybe The Incredible Hulk?"

"Henry," I gasped, "is it really you? I don't understand."

What Jackyl told me was in the strictest confidence. I vowed never to breath a word of it to a living soul. I even promised not to sell the story to the Enquirer which would have paid me a handsome sum.

Chapter VIII

JACKYL'S NARRATIVE

Jackyl resembled a man returned from the dead as he spoke in a tired voice. "Sigmoid, I have always been convinced that twin natures inhabited our bodies, one good and one evil. Through my long countless experiments I discovered certain chemicals that separated the two elements."

"But Henry, why didn't you try it on laboratory animals?" I asked.

"I did and my goldfish attacked me. So I drank the potion myself and I became another person—Mr. High! He was evil, he knocked down children and old ladies. He smoked in non-smoking sections of public places. He put whoopee cushions on the benches in church! He scratched his private parts in public! He picked his nose in four star restaurants! He walked his dog without a pooper scooper! He left his chewing gum on the arm rest of the chairs in the theatre and he'd talk and crinkle candy wrappers throughout the entire movie! And he refuses to stand up when they play 'God Save the Queen'."

"The <u>bounder</u>! You're right, Jackyl, he's evil, pure evil!"

Chapter IX

JACKYL'S PROMISE

Jackyl looked at me and said in a firm voice, "I'm through with High. Just look at what he does to my trousers! They're terribly wrinkled. You have my word old chum, High is gone forever, scout's honor."

"That's alright for you to say," I replied, "but High owes me for <u>two sessions!</u>"

"I'll gladly pay," smiled Jackyl.

"I should charge you double, since I was doing 'couple's' therapy without even knowing it!"

Jackyl rose to leave and said, "Sigmoid, I really must go. I resolve to devote the rest of my life to doing good deeds and charity work."

"Bravo!" I cried. "That's splendid and it's also a great way to beat the ruddy income tax!"

Chapter X

THE RETURN OF MR. HIGH

Jackyl was true to his word. He literally threw himself into his good works. He opened a free medical clinic for the disadvantaged and even had informative magazines like Playboy and the Star in his waiting room. It was as if High never existed.

One morning as I was walking to my office, I heard the shout of a newspaper vendor, "HEXTRY HEXTRY, HREAD HALL HABOUT HIT! SIR GUY MURDERED!"

I purchased a paper and read the grim news. Sir Guy Fawkes Pigot Smith Stratford on Avon, member of the House of Lords, was brutally murdered by a short, repulsive bloke in an ill-fitting suit. It was reported that as the fiend beat Sir Guy about the head with his cane he had been shouting "Though I've belted you and flayed you, by the livin' gawd that made you, you're a better man than I am, Gunga Din."

"Hm," I mused half aloud, "I had no idea that Mr. High was fond of Kipling."

I heard a familiar voice say, "I didn't even know he kippled." It was Henry Jackyl.

" Jackyl," I said, "I'm glad to see you haven't lost your sense of humor in light of what has happened. But I must say I'm terribly disturbed over Mr. High's latest peccadillo."

Chapter XI

A MURDERER SURRENDERS

Jackyl and I stepped into a shop for some tea. "Sigmoid, I think I'm going mad," said he. "Perhaps you ought to commit me to an asylum!"

"An asylum? What is it?"

"You know, a place where they keep dingalings," said Jackyl.

"No, I mean, what's wrong, Henry? Why after you gave me your word, has that dreadful Mr. High reappeared?"

Jackyl sighed, "I can no longer control High! He comes and goes as he wishes, and as for me, I don't know whether I'm coming or going! Last night I went to bed Dr. Jackyl and I awoke as High and now…" His voice trailed off, finally he continued, "…and now I'm a murderer! I have no choice, I'm going to turn myself into Scotland Yard!"

"I say, that's extraordinary. I know that you can turn yourself into High, but Scotland Yard? How do you do that?" I inquired.

"No," returned Jackyl, "I mean I'm going to surrender to the Yard."

"Good show, Henry," I applauded.

The next morning, it wasn't Dr. Jackyl who appeared at Scotland Yard and turned himself in, it was Mr. High!

Chapter XII

THE TRIAL OF EDWARD HIGH

The trial was held in the Old Bailey with Judge Ty A. Noose (the hanging judge), presiding.

The first witness for the crown was the constable who had found the body. He described the despicable act that had killed Sir Guy. The jury shuddered as he raised High's splintered cane. "This is the very weapon," said the constable, "that crushed poor Sir Guy's 'ead!"

The following day, seven eye witnesses to the brutal crime were scheduled to testify. The situation looked grim indeed for Mr. High.

That night the guards placed High in his cell and locked him in. When they woke him to appear in court the next morning, they were shocked by his changed appearance. He looked like an entirely different man. Actually, he was. It was Henry Jackyl. The guards swore that the prisoner had been under constant surveillance and they had never left their posts.

None of the witnesses could identify the man in the dock as the murderer. The jury had no choice but to find Mr. High, "Not guilty."

I never laid eyes on Jackyl or High again! After the trial they simply <u>disappeared</u>!

Then one day I chanced upon a notice in the press that Lady D., a distant relative of the Queen had married a Mr. Edward High. It has long been rumored that she was into the leather and S and M scene (her ladyship, that is, not the Queen).

A week later an even more shocking incident occurred. A man was killed in the bed chamber of Lady D. According to the account in the Enquirer, Lady D. and her husband, Edward, had retired for the night. When she woke up in the morning, her husband was gone and a strange man was in her bed. Her Ladyship started to scream and her servants rushed to her assistance. In the ensuing melee, the intruder was shot and killed. He was later identified as Dr. Henry Jackyl!

Nobody ever saw High nor hair again!*

*Several noted experts on genetics share the opinion that the physical and mental resemblances between <u>Mr. High</u> and <u>Mick Jagger</u> are more than coincidental, and that the rock star may very well indeed be a direct descendant of <u>High himself</u>!

A MAD LOOK AT IGOR

No feel bad, girls turn Igor down, too! Know why?
Because we dress like slobs! Come, Igor fix!
MAD

153

GLOVES

$30 PAIR

MR BIG
GUY
BUSINESS
SUIT

DANDY
LONG
LEGS

BIG
FOOT-
RIGHT
LINE

LATEST
ARM
WHERE
THE
HEAD
SHOULD
BE
LINE

3 AND 5 SLEEVED
SHIRTS THIS WAY

4 LEGGED
MAN
LINE

155

157

159

161

CAMP SLEEP-AWAY

I don't wanna go to any dumb, ol' **camp!**

You'll have a lot of **fun**…

It's **boring!** Making stupid wallets, roasting marshmallows—all that **garbage!** The kids are all **wimps** and the counselors are **nerds!**

That's not true! Your **dad** went to Camp Sleep-A-Way when he was your age, and later he was a **counselor** there!

Case closed!

We've already paid! You're **going!** Like you said—**case closed!**

166

Yes, we're trying to get to **Camp Sleep-A-Way,** and this character started raving about **Druids...**
Don't pay him no mind! That's **Crazy Ezra!** He owns the local stereo store.
And my prices are **insane!**
Among other things!

You take Route 25 and get off at Exit 64! It's about five miles, next to the cemetery!
He said **"curse!"**
Oh, you'll hear plenty of **4-letter words!** That's what camps teach kids!
No, I mean the **"Curse of the Druids!"**

171

Simon Says the game's over! Gosh, wasn't that **fun?** How do you like camp so far?
IT SUCKS!

No, that's a **nice** name! They called me **Yellow-stain** because I **wet the bed!** The counselors just **laughed,** So I **killed** them!
But that was **10 years** ago! **We** didn't have anything to do with **that!**
You're a **counselor,** aintcha? You're **all** the same!
Why did you come back here?
I never left! It was kinda lonely, but it beats goin' to school!

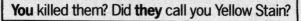

You killed them? Did **they** call you Yellow Stain?

No, they called me **'Chooch'**—and I'm not even Italian!

That's nothing! My dad calls my boy friend **'Shmuck',** and we're not Jewish! Damien why don't you stop all this killing! You can join our staff—we have several vacancies! You can show the campers how to use an **ax!**

Nahh, they'd just make fun of me! But enough talking! I have to **kill you!**

185

Are you alright?
I'm okay—is he . . . ?
He's dead! That spear went right through his —
- heart!
Grrrrah!
Holy Stephen King—he's **not** dead!

189

Well, how was camp?
Neat, dad, **real neat!** I can't wait to go back **next year!**